JERSEY
IN OLD PHOTOGRAPHS

EDWARDIAN BATHING BELLES standing beside bathing machines. These wooden structures on substantial wheels were a familiar feature on the more popular beaches, notably Grève d'Azette, West Park, First Tower, Millbrook and St Brelade's. (Early this century.)

JERSEY
IN OLD PHOTOGRAPHS

COLLECTED BY
RAOUL LEMPRIERE

ALAN SUTTON
1987

Alan Sutton Publishing Limited
Brunswick Road · Gloucester

First published 1987

British Library Cataloguing in Publication Data

Jersey in old photographs.
1. Jersey—History
I. Lempriere, Raoul
942.3′41082   DA670.J5

ISBN 0-86299-404-7

Typesetting and origination by
Alan Sutton Publishing Limited
Printed in Great Britain
by WBC Print Ltd · Bristol

CONTENTS

'THE WHITE COONS' – one of the concert parties which visited Jersey during the summer season and performed in the Triangle Park (or if wet or cold in West Park Pavilion), St Helier. (Early this century.)

INTRODUCTION

Interest in old photographs has greatly increased during recent years and instead of being thoughtlessly thrown away, they are now in many cases carefully preserved and reproduced in books, magazines and newspapers, recalling to those who see them a way of life now only a memory and for some not even that.

The selection of photographs in this book is with very few exceptions drawn from my collection of photographs, postcards and books made over some forty years, and spans the period c. 1870–1938.

In order to appreciate and fully understand the photographs it is necessary to know a little about Jersey and its way of life during the period represented.

Jersey has an area of forty-five square miles and is the largest of the Channel Islands, the most southerly of the British Isles. At the closest point it is about fifteen miles from the west coast of Normandy.

Jersey is a Bailiwick comprising the main island and a number of islets, notably the Ecréhous and the Minquiers. At the beginning of the period it had a population of (1871 census) 56,627 and at the end (1931 census) 50,455.

The island is divided into 12 ancient parishes each of which is an administrative district presided over by a Constable (Mayor). The capital is the town of Saint Helier which lies approximately halfway along the south coast, occupies a large part of the parish of the same name and overspills into neighbouring parishes.

The Sovereign is represented by a Lieutenant-Governor. The Chief Magistrate and President of the States Assembly (the legislature) is the Bailiff before whom in the Royal Court, in the States and on special occasions is carried the magnificent silver-gilt mace. This was presented to Jersey by King Charles II, as a proof of his royal affection towards the island in which he had been twice received in safety during the Civil War when he was excluded from the remainder of his dominions.

The photographs are divided into eight sections dealing respectively with The Town of Saint Helier and its Suburbs, Coast and Country, Agriculture, Transport, The Garrison and the Royal Militia Island of Jersey, Summer Pastimes, People and Events.

Saint Helier like most other towns during the period had many small privately-owned shops the proprietors of which, more often than not, 'lived over the shop'. 'The Town', as it was commonly called, was the hub of the island with the seat of government, the Royal Court House, the markets, the principal shops, the leading hotels, numerous public houses and the main harbour. It was quite large and had increased greatly in size since the beginning of the nineteenth century.

The coast and country were wholly unspoilt. There were the 12 ancient parish churches, water-mills and windmills, beautiful granite farmhouses, a number of fine mansions, little old cottages, many of them thatched, a number of hotels and public houses, and many fortifications dating from the thirteenth to the nineteenth century.

The principal industry was agriculture, particularly the growing and exporting of 'Jersey Royal' potatoes, and, to a lesser extent, the rearing and exporting of the beautiful Jersey cattle, still the only breed allowed on the island.

The island was traversed by a number of main roads, many of them originally built for military purposes, and innumerable narrow winding lanes bordered by high banks and overhung with trees. There were, until almost the end of the period, two railways, one which ran from Saint Helier to Corbière and the other from Saint Helier to Gorey Pier. Communication with the outside world was solely by sea, mainly through the Port of Saint Helier, until the advent of a regular air service in the 1930s.

Down the centuries Britain had maintained a garrison in Jersey and was to continue to do so until 1926. In addition there was the Royal Militia, one of the most ancient forces of the Crown, of which the island was immensely proud.

Ever since peace had descended on Europe in 1815, Jersey was visited each year by ever increasing numbers of visitors and by the end of the century was to have a substantial tourist industry which continued growing to the end of the period and beyond. This accounted for the large number of hotels and guest houses in the island, the excursion cars with their guides, the summer shows at the theatre and in the Triangle Park and much else besides.

During the period farmers and country people were principally of old Jersey stock and still for the most part spoke Jersey Norman-French, as well as English. In the town of Saint Helier, in addition to the local people, many families were to be found, mostly from the United Kingdom, some of whom had been established only for a generation or two, or who had recently settled there. There were also a number of French families who had taken up residence since 1815. In addition there was a considerable non-native resident population, consisting largely of retired naval and army officers, who, with the principal native families and the officers of the garrison, formed their own social circles.

And as for 'Events' – they were much as elsewhere although the Battle of Flowers dating from 1902 and a few other occasions, particularly those relating to the Royal Militia, could be claimed to be local.

Despite the Boer Wars and the Great War, the period was one of stability and gradual change. The framework of life was well established. The family was the unit in which people lived. There was discipline in the home, at school, at work and in honorary service whether in the States, in the parishes or in the Royal Militia. Church-going was the rule rather than the exception. Despite a hard lifestyle, with none of the present day labour-saving devices, and a certain amount of poverty, many were able to gain a great deal of enjoyment and satisfaction out of life. So that those who are old enough to recall any of the people, places and events depicted here will almost certainly do so with affectionate remembrance rather than the contrary.

At the beginning of the period there were a number of well established photographers in Jersey, notably Thomas Tibbles, R. Eager, C.P. Ouless, and E. Baudoux & Son, who were to be followed by, among others, J. Simonton, A. Laurens, Albert Smith (successor to E. Baudoux & Son), E. Hamilton Toovey, Tynan Bros. (late of E. Baudoux & Son) and de Beer & Lloyd. In addition there were the postcard photographers such as F. Foot and the well-known Louis Levy ('L.L.'), and numerous amateur photographers. The work of professional photographers, postcard photographers and amateurs, in particular Leonard Cutbush, is represented in this book.

I would take this opportunity to thank Mr Clifford Le Clercq for supplying three of the photographs and preparing the whole collection for publication, and Mr B.J. Bevis for permission to reproduce the photograph of Down's bus. I would also place on record my sincere appreciation of the assistance so readily given to me by Mr Robin Cox, Mr Kevin Le Scelleur, Mr Winston Le Brun and Mr Tony Watton, as well as by Miss C. Easterbrook and Miss C. Jurd of the Jersey Public Library, Reference Department. Finally, I would thank the members of my staff who typed the introduction and the captions.

RAOUL LEMPRIERE
Jersey, 27 July, 1987

LADY OTWAY (ob. 1910), one of the leaders of island society, standing beside her harp. Her residence, Gloucester House, Rouge Bouillon, St Helier, was the centre of all that was 'distinguished socially and artistically'.

The Town of Saint Helier and its Suburbs

THE ROYAL SQUARE, the heart of the town, prior to the building of the Public Library. On the left is to be seen part of the Royal Court with the statue of King George II in front of it and St Helier's parish church in the distance towards the right. (Before 1887.)

THE ROYAL SQUARE, after the building of the Public Library. (Between 1887 and early in 1894.)

HALKETT PLACE looking north. The old market on the east side of the street had been demolished prior to rebuilding. Opposite may be seen the premises of J.T. Baker, Chemist, at No. 25 displaying the customary red lamp. The decorative arches were erected for the centenary of the Battle of Jersey. (January 1881.)

HALKETT PLACE looking north with the French Wesleyan Chapel (now called Wesley-Grove Church) at the far end and the Halkett Hotel in the right foreground. (Early this century.)

'THE RED LION', Halkett Place. The fine sign and the lamp have long since gone but the building remains. (January 1881.)

HALKETT PLACE looking south towards its junction with Queen Street to the left and King Street to the right, and the small thoroughfare known as Morier Lane straight ahead. Mrs W.H. Slater's corner shop sold a wide range of goods including stationery, books and newspapers. (January 1881.)

HALKETT PLACE looking south with the States' Chamber in the distance on the right. A 'Le Riche's' horse-drawn van is to be seen on the left. (In or before 1909.)

W.H. MILNE'S PIANOFORTE ROOMS, 37 Halkett Place. (In or before 1907.)

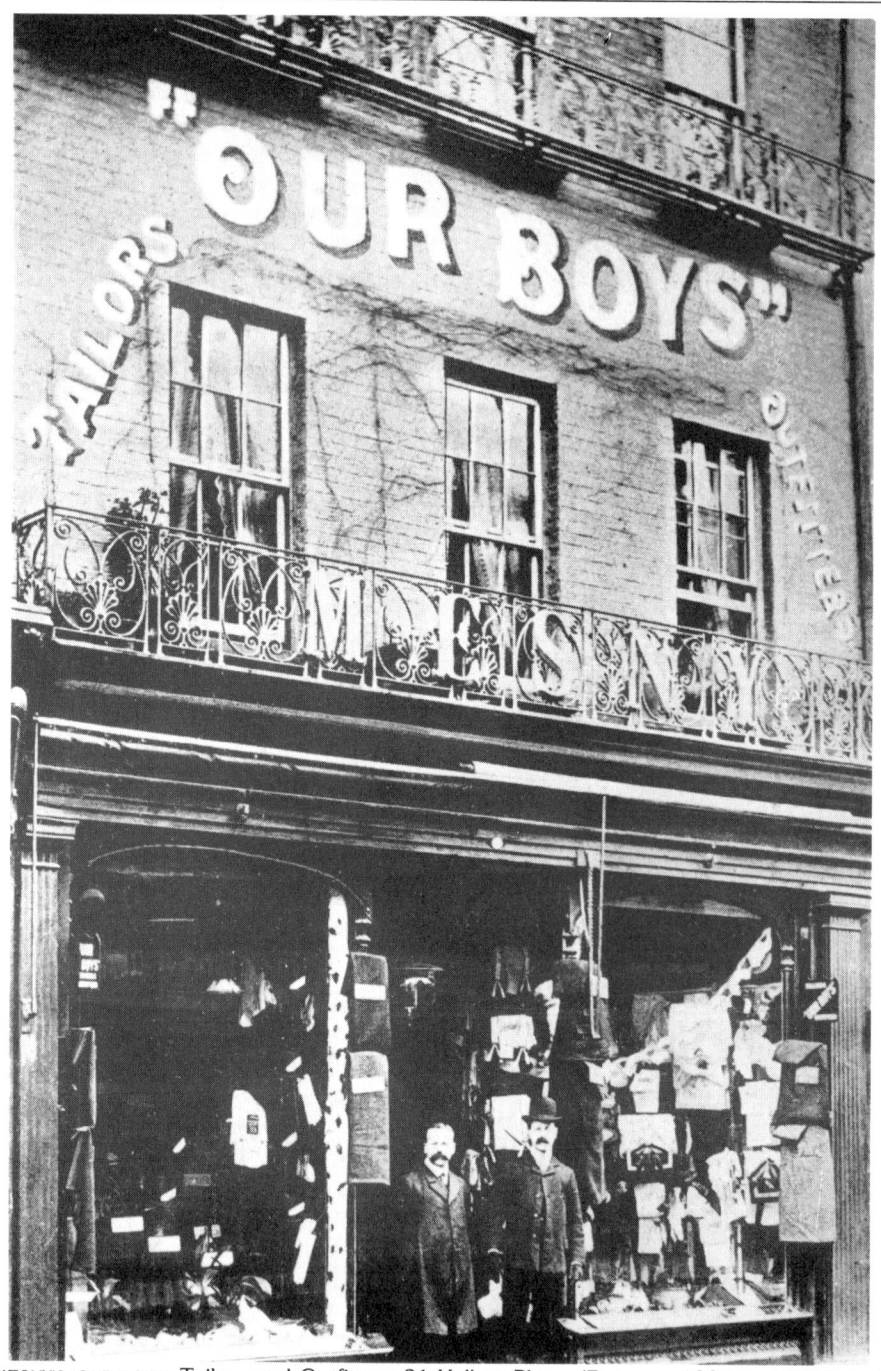

MESNY'S 'OUR BOYS', Tailors and Outfitters, 31 Halkett Place. (Between 1901 and 1909.)

THE KATOOKELLA TEA WAREHOUSE, 'purveyors of Ceylon's finest teas', 55 Halkett Place. (Early this century.)

THE NEW MARKET (bearing the date 1881 on its Halkett Place frontage), forming the corner of Beresford Street and Halkett Place, with a glimpse of the Victoria Club on the left of the picture. (Early this century.)

THE INTERIOR OF THE NEW MARKET. The attractive fountain is to be seen on the left of the picture. (Early this century.)

T.L. DE FAYE, Family Butcher (established 1821), 14 and 15 the New Market. (In or before 1897.)

F. COLEMAN, Wine & Spirit Merchant, 2 Beresford Street. (In or before 1897.)

BERESFORD STREET showing part of the New Market on the right with the Victoria Club, 'the *rendezvous* of officers and the élite', beyond. In front of the New Market is a carriage stand. (In or before 1903.)

GELLENDER'S BOOT STORE (established 1813), 9 Beresford Street (facing Victoria Club). (In or before 1909.)

AUSTRALIAN HERBAL STORES, on the corner of Bath Street and Hillgrove Street. Probably H. Trueblood, the proprietor, standing in the doorway. (Not earlier than 1926).

BROAD STREET AND THE LE SUEUR OBELISK. The building on the left of the picture was The Capital and Counties Bank. The third building to the right of the obelisk (in the middle distance) was occupied by J. Lewis, Hairdresser, (c. 1883).

THE ABC TEA ROOMS, 39 Broad Street. There was a branch in Bath Street and another in Cattle Street. (Early this century.)

MERCANTILE HOTEL, 11 Broad Street. (Early this century.)

THE ROYAL YACHT HOTEL (established at least as early as the 1820s), Caledonia Place, and P. McAllen's Elephant and Castle Hotel forming the corner of Mulcaster Street and Wharf Street, (c. 1895).

W.F. RENOUF, Ironmonger, 22 Burrard Street. (Early this century.)

AURORA HOTEL, 7 & 8 Cattle Street. (In or before 1897.)

DAVID PLACE looking north with Brée's Royal Hotel (formerly the Stopford Hotel) on the right and St Mark's Church beyond. (In or before 1908.)

LARBALESTIER, Eau-de-Cologne Manufacturer (established 1813). In 1847 Philippe Larbalestier, then of 45 Broad Street, was appointed Manufacturer of Eau-de-Cologne in Ordinary to Queen Victoria. The Royal Warrant was signed by the Mistress of the Robes. (Early this century.)

HÔTEL DE LA BOULE D'OR, Conway Street. One of a number of French hotels established in Saint Helier between 1815 and the end of the century. (Early this century.)

DON ROAD DAIRY & DON ROAD STORES, 16 Don Road and 1, 3 & 5 Francis Street, were well known for many years as dairymen and grocers. (After 3 October 1927.)

ROYAL CRESCENT CHAPEL, Don Road, occupying the site of the Theatre Royal, destroyed by fire in 1865. The chapel has been demolished and the site remains vacant. (Early this century.)

'PLAISANCE'. Don Road. The house was demolished and the property converted into the 'Howard Davis Park', opened 30 September 1939.

POMME D'OR HÔTEL, Esplanade. Another of the French hotels. (Early this century.)

POMME D'OR HÔTEL GARDEN. Advertised as 'A glimpse of Paris life in Jersey'. (Early this century.)

THE GRAND HOTEL, Esplanade. (1890 – by T.E. Colcutt.) (In or before 1905.)

THE GRAND HOTEL – part of the lounge. (In or before 1914.)

THEATRE ROYAL, Gloucester Street – interior. The building was destroyed by fire on 29 March 1899. (In or before 1897.)

THEATRE ROYAL, Gloucester Street – exterior and interior depicted on a programme cover. (Probably 1898.)

THE OPERA HOUSE, Gloucester Street, built on the site of the Theatre Royal. (Early this century.)

THE OPERA HOUSE — interior. (Before 12 May 1921.)

OPERA HOUSE
JERSEY

MONDAY, FEB. 3rd, 1902
AND TWO FOLLOWING NIGHTS.

Mr. Calder O'Beirne

Presents his specially selected Company of **IRISH PLAYERS**, including the CELEBRATED IRISH COMEDIAN

JOHN S. CHAMBERLAIN

(Of Theatres Royal, Drury Lane, Adelphi, and Princess')

The "Freeman's Journal," March 19th, 1900, says — "Such a sterling Artiste as Mr. John S. Chamberlain, one of the best, if indeed not absolutely the very best Irish Comedian, of which the stage can boast of to-day."

MONDAY, February 3rd.

DION BOUCICAULT'S Famous Irish Drama, in Three Acts —

— THE — SHAUGHRAUN

Act 1, Scene 1—**SUILABEG.** Scene 2—**THE BLASKETS.** Scene 3—Exterior of Father Dolan's. Scene 4—Home of the Parish Priest. Act 2, Scene 1—A ROOM IN BALLYRAGGET HOUSE. Scene 2—Father Dolan's. Scene 3—The Barrack Room. Scene 4—Mrs. O'Kelly's Cabin. Scene 5—**THE GATE TOWER.** Scene 6—**THE BLASKETS.** Scene 7—Rathgarron Head. Scene 8—Ruins of St. Bridget's Abbey. Act 3, Scene 1—**MRS. O'KELLY'S CABIN.** Scene 2—**THE WAKE OF CONN THE SHAUGHRAUN.** Scene 3—The Shanty. Scene 4—**THE COOT'S NEST.**

Tuesday, BOUCICAULT'S ROMANTIC IRISH DRAMA—

ARRAH-NA-POGUE
OR, THE WICKLOW WEDDING

Act 1—Glendalough. Act 2—The Justice Hall. Act 3—The Watch Tower

Wednesday,
BOUCICAULT'S MASTERPIECE—

COLLEEN BAWN

Act 1—**TORC CREGAN.** Road to Garryowen. Limerick is beautiful. Kitty O'Connor's Cottage. Crawkeen Lawn. **THE OATH.** Act 2—GROUNDS OF TORC CREGAN. Library of Castle Chute. Slieveh's Cottages. The Pretty Girl Milking her Cow. Myles-na-Coppaleen, with Songs. Limerick v Benefit! and "Pot Malice." Act 3—SHEILAH'S COTTAGE. **THE GREAT WATER CAVE.** Act 4—INTERIOR OF SHEILAH'S COTTAGE. Death of Danny Mann. Ruins in Torc Cregan. **ILLUMINATED GARDENS OF TORC CREGAN.**

PRICES OF ADMISSION:

Private Boxes, 21s.; Orchestra Stalls (Bonnets not allowed), 3s. 6d.; Dress Circle (Bonnets not allowed), 3s.; Second Stalls, 2s. (if booked in advance or Early Doors, 2s. 6d.); Upper Circle, 1s. (if booked in advance or Early Doors, 1s. 6d.); Pit, 1s., or Early Doors, 1s. 6d.; Gallery, 6d. or Early Doors, 9d.

ALL SEATS (except Pit and Gallery) can be Booked in advance at THE BERESFORD LIBRARY (TELEPHONE No. 196).
TIME OF OPENING :—Early Doors at 7.20. Ordinary Doors at 7.40. CURTAIN TO RISE AT 8 O'CLOCK.
Musical Conductor, Mr. A. McKEE. Master Carpenter, Mr. JOHN LE CRAS. Scenic Artist, Mr. HENRY SIDNEY.

The Jersey Railways & Tramways Ltd. will run Opera House Trains, on Tuesday and Thursday, leaving St. Helier's at 10.45. The Jersey Eastern Railway Co. will run an Opera House Train, leaving Snow Hill at 11.15 o'clock each Thursday.

THE OPERA HOUSE – poster with times of the 'theatre trains' printed at the bottom. (1902.)

'THE LONDON PLAYERS' photographed outside the Opera House. (1925.)

A.A. BALL, Devonshire Dairy, 59 Great Union Road. Part of a milk cart is to be seen on either side of the picture. (Early this century.)

HAVRE-DES-PAS – the bathing pool (inaugurated 1895) viewed from the landward end of the bridge. (Early this century.)

INSTITUTION NOTRE DAME DE BON SECOURS (now the premises of Highlands College), Highlands Lane, St Saviour. Rising up behind the right-hand section of the building is to be seen the 'Eiffel Tower' at Maison St Louis Observatory, demolished in 1929. (Early this century.)

KING STREET looking east showing from the left J.A. Malzard, Tobacconist, Brooks, Booksellers & Stationers, and in the middle distance, de Gruchy's Department Store; on the right La Belle Jardinière, Fancy Repository. (In or before 1905.)

VOISIN & CO. (established 1837) – King Street frontage with Gaudins (part of the same firm) occupying the shop on the left of the picture. The premises were decorated for the visit of King George V and Queen Mary. (July 1921.)

KING STREET looking west showing on the left Hamon & Son, Drapers, Victoria House, on the corner of Brook Street, and on the right R.B. Colley & Co., Tailors. (In or before 1905.)

THE LONDON JEWELLERS & SILVERSMITHS CO., forming the corner of King Street and Brook Street. (In or before 1897.)

A. DE GRUCHY & CO. LTD. (established 1810), 46, 48, 50 & 52 King Street. (Early this century.)

LA COLLETTE. The house peeping out through the trees on the right of the picture has been demolished. (Early this century.)

GREGORY'S ROYAL LIVERY STABLES, 49 La Motte Street, provided the carriages used by Queen
Victoria and Prince Albert when they visited Jersey in 1846 and again in 1859, hence the
Royal Arms displayed on the front of the premises, (c. 1870.).

VICTORIA COLLEGE, Mont Millais. The main building before the construction of the quadrangle. (Early this century.)

VICTORIA COLLEGE – the physics laboratory. (Early this century.)

HÔTEL DE L'EUROPE, Mulcaster Street – another of the French hotels. The next building along housed Bellingham's ocean and rail travel office. (Early this century.)

HÔTEL DE L'EUROPE – the dining room. (In or before 1915.)

LOOKING EAST ALONG LIBRARY PLACE. In the forefront of the picture, on the left, forming the corner of New Cut, is the Commercial Bank (now National Westminster Bank), and in the middle distance on the same side is the London, City & Midland Bank (now the Midland Bank). (In or before 1910.)

ST PAUL'S CHURCH (built 1815; demolished 1889), New Street. This was the forerunner of the present building opened in 1891. (In or before 1889.)

EDWARD LEE & SON, Musical Instrument Repository, 22 New Street. (Early this century.)

THE PARADE. At the centre of the picture is the bust of Philippe Baudains, Constable (Mayor) of St Helier (1881–96) on a granite plinth within railings. (In or before 1922.)

E. HAMILTON TOOVEY, Photographic Artist, Don View Studio, 36 Parade. (In or before 1897.)

THE ROYAL HALL, Peter Street. A cinema was established there in 1909 by T.J. West. The building was demolished and the site incorporated in a purpose built cinema erected after World War One. (Early this century.)

QUEEN STREET, north side, looking towards the west. (Early this century.)

QUEEN STREET, south side, showing the Exeter public house, the second property from the left. The Continental Hotel protrudes beyond the building line considerably narrowing the width of the thoroughfare. (Early this century.)

GEORGE D. LAURENS, Basket and Rope Manufacturer and General Merchant, 3 Queen Street. (Early this century.)

BASKET MAKERS AT WORK with baskets stacked behind them. (Early this century.)

P.J. DU HEAUME, Family Baker and Confectioner, 20 Queen Street. (In or before 1905.)

JERSEY MODERN SCHOOL, Rouge Bouillon. A cricket match in progress. (In or before 1906.)

W.C. WHITE, Model Steam Bakery, St Mark's Road – exterior. (In or before 1896.)

W.C. WHITE, Model Steam Bakery, St Mark's Road – interior. (In or before 1896.)

JAMES HARPER. Springfield Nursery, 2 Trinity Road. (In or before 1897.)

ST THOMAS'S CHURCH, Val Plaisant – 'Maria Immaculata' bell – first rung on 8 December, 1904. (In or before 1905.)

VALLÉE-DES-VAUX (Ducks' Valley), St Helier. (Early this century.)

VICTORIA DAIRY, Victoria Street – horse-drawn cart and hand-carts in front of the dairy. The hand-carts contain the traditional Jersey milk cans made of tin plate. (In or before 1895.)

YORK HOTEL, Vine Street. (Between 1894 and 1897.)

THE WEIGHBRIDGE showing the Weighbridge Gardens before the erection of Queen Victoria's Statue at their centre. The entrance to the railway terminus was rebuilt in 1901, the Westaway Memorial was removed to the Victoria Pier in 1888 and the Southampton Hotel was rebuilt in 1899. (July 1883.)

LOOKING SOUTH ACROSS THE WEIGHBRIDGE to the harbour with Commercial Buildings bordering it on the left and Fort Regent dominating the scene. In the forefront of the picture may be seen the Westaway Memorial. (July 1883.)

Coast and Country

ELIZABETH CASTLE, St Aubin's Bay, showing the causeway connecting it with West Park slipway, St Helier. (Early this century.)

BELLOZANNE VALLEY, St Helier, with a distant view of First Tower, St Aubin's Bay and Noirmont Headland. (In or before 1887.)

ST BRELADE'S BAY in the parish of the same name. On the left is to be seen St Brelade's Church and in the distance, towards the right, St Brelade's Bay Hotel. Unlike today the hinterland is bare with scarcely a house in sight. (Late last century or early this century.)

ST PETER'S WINDMILL, St Peter. (In or before 1905.)

ST BRELADE'S CHURCH – one of Jersey's ancient parish churches. It is depicted here before its restoration 1895–1900. The sash window at the west end has been replaced by a doorway and a similar window to the right has been replaced by a window more in keeping with the building. (Probably late 1880s.)

L'ETACQ, ST OUEN. The woman is wearing a Jersey sun-bonnet and pushing a wheelbarrow with slatted sides designed to carry seaweed. (In or before 1904.)

L'ETACQ, ST OUEN. The tower was demolished during the German Occupation 1940–45 and replaced by a concrete bunker. (Early this century.)

PLEMONT, ST OUEN, showing the waterfall. This bay is known for the Needle Rock and a number of caves. (Early this century.)

VINCHELEZ LANE, St Ouen. On the left of the picture is a granite archway giving access to the grounds of Vinchelez de Bas Manor. (July 1883.)

ST JOHN'S HOTEL in the parish of the same name. The building has been demolished and replaced by a public house. (In or after 1923.)

ST JOHN'S HOTEL – the dining room. (In or after 1923.)

ROZEL HARBOUR, Trinity, with Rozel Fort on the headland to the right. (Early this century.)

'LA CHAIRE', ROZEL, ST MARTIN. Towards the end of the last century the house pictured here, built by Samuel Curtis, was replaced by a larger one, now converted into a hotel. At one time the property was renowned for its garden. (In or before 1887.)

A THATCHED COTTAGE, Rozel, St Martin. (In or before 1907.)

THE LODGE at the head of St Catherine's Breakwater, St Martin. (Early this century.)

LES ECRÉHOUS – a group of islets lying between the east coast of Jersey and the west coast of Normandy, and considered part of the parish of St Martin. A primitive stone cottage and outbuildings long since gone. (1882 or 1883.)

A THATCHED COTTAGE AT ARCHIRONDEL, St Martin, with St Catherine's Breakwater in the distance. (In or before 1906.)

HUNT'S TEA AND REFRESHMENT ROOM, Gorey. The notice under the facia offers lemonade and ginger beer for sale. High up in the distance is to be seen the spire and tower of Gouray Church. (Early this century.)

A FISHERY PROTECTION VESSEL in Gorey harbour. (Early this century.)

MONT ORGUEIL CASTLE (generally known as Gorey Castle) with the harbour below and the 'Pierview Inn' to the right, just below centre. The picture was taken before the railway and the coast road were extended to Gorey Pier. (In or before 1887.)

PRINCE'S TOWER – a gazebo built c. 1780 by James d'Auvergne on top of La Hougue Bie (a neolithic passage grave covered by a huge mound of earth and rubble) and incorporating two ancient chapels. It became known as 'Prince's Tower' when it was inherited by the builder's nephew Philippe d'Auvergne who became Prince of Bouillon. The tower was demolished in 1924. (In or before 1887.)

PRINCE'S TOWER – the building in the grounds where luncheons, teas and other refreshments were provided. (In or before 1905.)

THE CHÂLET HOTEL, Pontac, St Clement. The establishment boasted among other amenities conservatories, gardens, a maze and floral nooks. (In or before 1910.)

NOs 2 & 3 MARINE TERRACE, St Clement. Victor Hugo lived at No. 3 during his stay in Jersey 1852–55. Both houses have now been demolished. (In or before 1905.)

GOVERNMENT HOUSE. St Saviour's Hill – the official residence of the Lieutenant-Governor. (In or before 1905.)

GOVERNMENT HOUSE – the Guard House. (In or before 1904.)

GRAINVILLE MANOR, St Saviour – the thatched lodge framed by trees. (In or before 1887.)

ST SAVIOUR'S CHURCH, St Saviour's Hotel, Saunders Cottage and the Parish Hall. The hotel and the cottage were demolished and the site of the two buildings was incorporated into the churchyard. (In or before 1909.)

OLD RECTORY, ST SAVIOUR – the birthplace of Lillie Langtry. Now a private house. (Early this century.)

SWISS VALLEY, St Saviour. (Early this century.)

TROGLODYTE CAVES, Five Oaks, St Saviour (opened 23 September, 1878) — arch erected to commemorate Queen Victoria's Golden Jubilee 1887. 'Caves' was a misnomer as they were really pleasure grounds constructed in disused clay-pits. (In or after 1892.)

TROGLODYTE CAVES – arch dated 1892 erected to the memory of the Prince Consort. (In or after 1892.)

TROGLODYTE CAVES – the lake with a model of a ship afloat. (In or after 1892.)

SECTION THREE

Agriculture

A CHAMPION JERSEY COW OF THE PERIOD. (In or before 1906.)

A COW BEING WATERED at a granite trough by a traditional Jersey well-head. (In or before 1906.)

A MILKMAID wearing a Jersey sun-bonnet and holding a traditional Jersey milking can, standing beside a cow in front of an old granite farm building. (In or before 1906.)

GATHERING SEAWEED, known locally as 'vraic'. The type of scene immortalized by the Jersey artist Edmund Blampied. (In or before 1903.)

PLOUGHING WITH THE 'BIG PLOUGH' drawn by six horses. (Early this century.)

HARVESTING THE POTATO CROP. The women are wearing Jersey sun-bonnets. (Early this century.)

JERSEY 'VANS' loaded with new potatoes at the Weighbridge, St Helier, at the height of the potato season. (Early this century.)

THE HARBOUR, St Helier – potatoes ready to be shipped to England. (Early this century.)

TWO WOMEN WEARING JERSEY SUN-BONNETS looking at some pigs. Many farmers kept pigs and local pork was considered very good. (Early this century.)

A WOMAN WEARING A JERSEY SUN-BONNET standing beside a patch of Jersey cabbages. The cabbage stalks were and are still dried and made into walking sticks. (In or before 1914.)

A GROUP TAKEN BY A THRESHING MACHINE. (In or after 1925.)

SECTION FOUR

Transport

A 'DOWN'S' HORSE-BUS which operated a service between Rouge Bouillon (Queen's Road) and Havre-des-Pas where it is pictured here. The driver was Thomas Richard Louden who died in 1930 aged 73. On the side of the vehicle are advertised de Faye's aerated table waters (1890s.)

A GROUP OF HOTEL HORSE-BUSES at the Harbour, St Helier, meeting the mailboat. At the top right of the picture may be seen Fort Regent and in the distance the town. (In or before 1902.)

PRIMROSE MOTOR COACH TOURS' FLEET OF COACHES lined up in Caledonia Place, St Helier. (1926.)

JERSEY RAILWAYS LIMITED, Terminus Building (1901), St Helier, with an excursion car on the point of departure. (In or before 1914.)

FIRST TOWER RAILWAY STATION (opened in 1870), St Helier. On the right of the picture may be seen 'First Tower' surmounted by a water tower. (Early this century.)

LA HAULE STATION (opened in 1876) – viewed from the road, looking east. (Early this century.)

LA HAULE RAILWAY STATION – viewed from the seaward side of the track. (Some time between 1906 and 1911.)

ST AUBIN'S TERMINUS HOTEL with the station to the rear. (Early this century.)

JERSEY EASTERN RAILWAY TERMINUS (opened 1874) St Helier. The station has long gone but the approach road from Hill Street, paved with granite setts, remains. (Early this century.)

ST AUBIN'S RAILWAY STATION and Terminus Hotel viewed from above the High Street on a sunny day. Both were severely damaged by fire on 18 October 1936. The hotel was repaired and is now St Brelade's Parish Hall. (In or before 1920.)

CORBIÈRE STATION – passengers alighting (c. 1908).

NO. 5 *'LA MOYE'* (built 1907; sold 1928) at Corbière Station (C. 1908).

GOREY VILLAGE STATION (opened in 1873; originally called Gorey Station and re-named in 1891). A number of national and local advertisements are displayed on the building and along the platform. Above the station to the right is to be seen Gouray Church. (In or before 1906.)

GOREY STATION (1891) with the harbour and castle. Along the Pier may be seen Cantell's British Hotel and Main's Elfine Hotel; also a number of horse-drawn vehicles. (Early this century.)

THE ENGINE *CALVADOS* (built 1872: scrapped c. 1927) with a stack of sleepers in the right foreground. (Last century.)

THE LONDON & SOUTH-WESTERN RAILWAY STEAMER *LAURA* (1885) passing Elizabeth Castle. (Early this century.)

THE GREAT WESTERN RAILWAY STEAMERS *ROEBUCK* (I) AND *REINDEER* moored side by side at the New North Quay, St Helier's Harbour, with Commercial Buildings in the background and Fort Regent brooding above. (In or before 1909.)

THE PADDLE STEAMER *CYGNE* about to set sail from Gorey Harbour (probably) for Carteret in Normandy. (Early this century.)

AIRCRAFT ON THE BEACH at West Park, St Helier, with the harbour, Fort Regent and South Hill in the distance. The beach served as an airport until the opening of the airport at St Peter in 1937.

The Garrison and the Royal Militia Island of Jersey

COMBINED BANDS OF THE FIRST EAST SURREY REGIMENT. (Between 1905 and 1908.)

THE SECOND BATTALION KING'S OWN ROYAL LANCASTER REGIMENT on church parade, St James's Street, St Helier. St James's Church is on the right of the picture. (Between 1908 and 1911.)

CONTINGENT FROM THE ROYAL MILITIA ISLAND OF JERSEY for the Coronation celebration in London. (1902.)

PRESENTATION OF MEDALS FOR LONG SERVICE to men of the Royal Militia Island of Jersey by Major-General H.S. Gough, CB, CMG, Lieutenant-Governor, in the Royal Square, St Helier. (1 October 1905.)

ROYAL MILITIA ISLAND OF JERSEY ARTILLERY. (Early this century.)

ROYAL MILITIA ISLAND OF JERSEY – C Company Second Battalion mobilized for active service. (1914–15.)

THE MILITIA BALL, Springfield, St Helier. (Late 1920s or early 1930s.)

Summer Pastimes

A POSTCARD SHOWING A MODESTLY DRESSED BATHING BELLE supporting a life belt with a view of Portelet Bay, St Brelade, inset. In the bay is to be seen the Ile au Guerdain topped by a small defensive tower. (In or before 1908.)

A GROUP OF CHILDREN ON THE BEACH at West Park, St Helier. Bathing machines are much in evidence. The West-End Bathing Co. Ltd. controlled the nearby Victoria Marine Lake opened in 1897. (In or before 1909.)

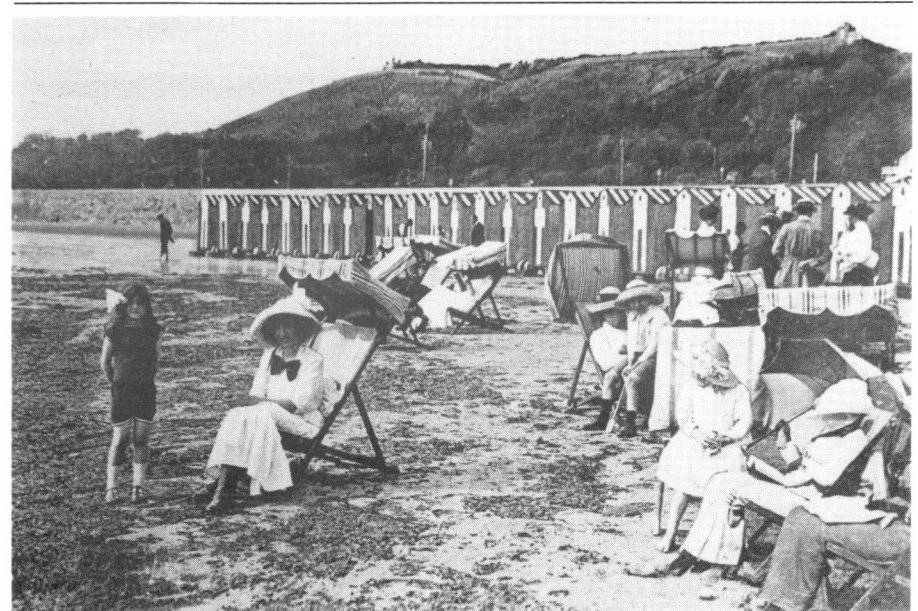

ON THE BEACH AT WEST PARK, St Helier. Bathing machines are much in evidence and Westmount is only partly covered with trees. (Early this century.)

A YOUNG WOMAN BEING CARRIED THROUGH THE CAVES at Plemont, St Ouen. (Early this century.)

A PICNIC PARTY at Corbière, St Brelade. (August 1910.)

TWO LADIES WITH A SLOW-WORM on a handkerchief at Corbière, St Brelade. (August 1910.)

THE PROMENADE AT WEST PARK, St Helier. Behind the bathing machines is to be seen West Park Pavilion, nicknamed the 'Tin Hunt', replaced in 1931 by a new building, now called 'The Inn on the Park'. (Early this century.)

A GROUP OF EXCURSION CARS drawn up outside the Victoria Hotel, St Peter's Valley, with some of the passengers relaxing in the road and in the field opposite. The Victoria Hotel has been rebuilt. (Between 1906 and 1911.)

THE PAVILION HOTEL, Grève de Lecq, St Ouen – a group of excursionists, some on their horse-drawn excursion car and others sitting or reclining in front. The man wearing the leather belt bearing the name 'Leo' was the guide (c. 1902).

A GROUP OF EXCURSIONISTS on a Gordon Benett's Paragon motor charabanc. (4 June 1920.)

LISTENING TO THE BAND in the Triangle Park, St Helier. The park has been re-named 'Victoria Park' and the bandstand has been demolished. (Early this century.)

LA ROCQUE REGATTA IN PROGRESS. (Early this century.)

'THE GAIETIES' – another of the concert parties which visited Jersey during the summer season and also performed in the Triangle Park, St Helier. (Early this century.)

THE BATTLE OF FLOWERS, Springfield, St Helier – Float 'HMS *Jersey*' entered by the St Helier Agricultural Society in the Parochial Class. It was complete with working telephone system, siren, signal bell, wireless, movable guns and searchlight, and won first prize. (28 July 1938.)

THE BATTLE OF FLOWERS — an exhibit on the road — probably on its way to Springfield. Up to World War I 'The Battle' was held on Victoria Avenue. When it was fully revived in 1928 it was held at Springfield. Today once again it is held on Victoria Avenue. (Between 1928 and 1939).

People

PHILIP JOHN OULESS (1817–85), the celebrated artist sitting at his easel.

WILLIAM WYBERT ROUSBY (ob. 1907) aged 72 years, actor and manager of the Theatre Royal, Gloucester Street, St Helier, for over thirty years.

LILLIE LANGTRY (1853–1929), the 'Jersey Lily', who appeared in *The Degenerates*, the first production presented at the Opera House, Gloucester Street, St Helier.

THE VERY REVEREND SAMUEL FALLE, MA (1854–1937). A popular and much respected Dean of Jersey and Rector of St Helier.

A LITTLE EDWARDIAN TOWN GIRL in all her finery (c. 1907).

A YOUNG COUNTRY GIRL HOLDING A HEFFER and with a Jersey milkcan at her feet. (Early this century.)

A YOUNG WOMAN DRAWING WATER FROM A PUMP — a cat in attendance. (Early this century.)

FISHERMEN ON LES ECRÉHOUS. (Probably 1882 or 1883.)

JERSEY LADIES' COLLEGE (now Jersey College for Girls) – pupils with bicycles. (1905.)

ANCIENT ORDER OF FORESTERS COURT PROSPERITY NO. 1930. (Early this century.)

THE BOYS BRIGADE attached to St Thomas's Roman Catholic Church, Val Plaisant, St Helier. (Early this century.)

Events

THE UNVEILING OF THE STATUE OF GENERAL SIR GEORGE DON, Lieutenant-Governor of Jersey (1806–1814), The Parade, St Helier. (29 October 1885.)

ST AUBIN'S CHURCH – laying the foundation stone of the present building. The old church, now demolished, is to be seen on the left of the picture, (4 June 1889).

ST SAVIOUR'S PARISH HALL – laying the foundation stone. The Constable at the time was T. Le Gallais. (10 July 1890.)

THE UNVEILING OF QUEEN VICTORIA'S STATUE in the Weighbridge Gardens, St Helier. In 1976 the statue was removed to the Triangle Park, which was re-named Victoria Park. (3 September 1890.)

THE NEW MARKET, St Helier – the waters of the fountain transformed into cascades of ice. (January 1894.)

THE DIAMOND JUBILEE OF QUEEN VICTORIA — arch erected by the Society of Jersey Gardeners at Charing Cross, St Helier. (1897.)

DIAMOND JUBILEE OF QUEEN VICTORIA — arch erected by the Royal Jersey Agricultural Society at York Street, St Helier. (1897.)

DIAMOND JUBILEE OF QUEEN VICTORIA – arch erected by the freemasons at Cheapside, St Helier. (1897.)

THE FIRST BATTLE OF FLOWERS held in honour of the Coronation of King Edward VII and Queen Alexandra. The venue for the occasion was Victoria Avenue. (9 July 1902.)

DIAMOND JUBILEE OF QUEEN VICTORIA – arch designed and erected under the supervision of Edmund Berteau, the States' Engineer, at the entrance to Victoria Avenue, St Helier. (1897.)

INAUGURATION OF THE 'LORD ST HELIER', a Shand, Mason & Co. horse-drawn steam engine at a ceremony outside the Town Hall, York Street, St Helier. (31 July 1905.)

JERSEY LADIES' COLLEGE – Prizegiving. (1905.)

ST CLEMENT'S HORTICULTURAL SOCIETY'S 27TH ANNUAL SHOW, Samarès Manor, St Clement. (30 August 1906.)

PART OF THE FUNERAL PROCESSION OF MAJOR-GENERAL S.W.F.M. WILSON (1827–1907). (3 May 1907.)

RECEPTION OF THE VERY REVEREND SAMUEL FALLE, Dean of Jersey, by the Manchester Unity of Oddfellows (Jersey District). (23 October 1906.)

CONCOURS MUSICALE – some of the participants proceeding along Cheapside, St Helier. (May 1907.)

MONT ORGUEIL CASTLE handed over by the Crown to the States of Jersey. Major-General H.S. Gough, Lieutenant-Governor, and Sir William Vernon, Bailiff, leading the procession through the castle. (28 June 1907.)

MONT ORGUEIL CASTLE – a group photograph with the Lieutenant Governor and Bailiff seated in the front row, the Royal Mace held between them, and the halberdiers standing at the back. (28 June 1907.)

PROCLAMATION OF KING GEORGE V in the Royal Square, St Helier. The statue of King George II had been removed from its plinth for repair. (6 May 1910.)

CORONATION OF KING GEORGE V AND QUEEN MARY — York Street, St Helier. The Norman arch with turrets at the entrance to the Parade erected by the Coronation Fêtes Committee and decorated by the Society of Jersey Gardeners. (22 June 1911.)

ROEBUCK I being inspected by sightseers, having been beached in Saint Brelade's Bay after hitting the Kaines Reef off the south-west coast of the island on 19 July 1911.

ONE OF FOUR HYDRO-AEROPLANES which landed on the beach at West Park in a race from St Malo and back. These were the first aircraft to land in Jersey. (26 August 1912.)

VISIT OF KING GEORGE V, QUEEN MARY AND PRINCESS MARY TO JERSEY. Awaiting the Royal Procession as it proceeds eastwards along King Street, St Helier. (12 July 1921.)

SILVER JUBILEE OF KING GEORGE V – York Street, St Helier – archway erected by the Royal Jersey Agricultural & Horticultural Society. (1935.)

VISIT OF KING GEORGE V, QUEEN MARY AND PRINCESS MARY – The King inspecting the Officers' Training Corps in the Quadrangle of Victoria College. (12 July 1921.)

VISIT OF KING GEORGE V, QUEEN MARY AND PRINCESS MARY — The Royal Party leaves Mont Orgueil Castle. The school children of St Martin's Parish and the lads of the Jersey Home for Boys were grouped on the Green near the drawbridge. (12 July 1921.)

CAESAREA II lying partly submerged outside St Helier's Harbour with part of Elizabeth Castle and the Hermitage Rock in the background. (July 1923.)

SEAPLANE *CALCUTTA* AT JERSEY — The Rt. Hon. Sir Samuel Hoare, GBE, CMG, MP, being seen off by Major-General The Hon. Sir Francis Bingham, KCB, KCMG, Lieutenant-Governor, Lady Bingham and Sir William Vernon, KBE, Bailiff of Jersey. (29 May 1928.)

SILVER JUBILEE OF KING GEORGE V –
Queen Street, St Helier – archway
erected by the United Services Club.
(1935.)

SILVER JUBILEE OF KING GEORGE V – The Parade, St Helier – archway erected by the Battle of
Flowers Committee. (1935.)